I0468044

ISBN-13: 9781500290528

Dedicated in Loving Memory of

Aunt Virginia aka "Mama"

who met our Saviour on October 31, 2015

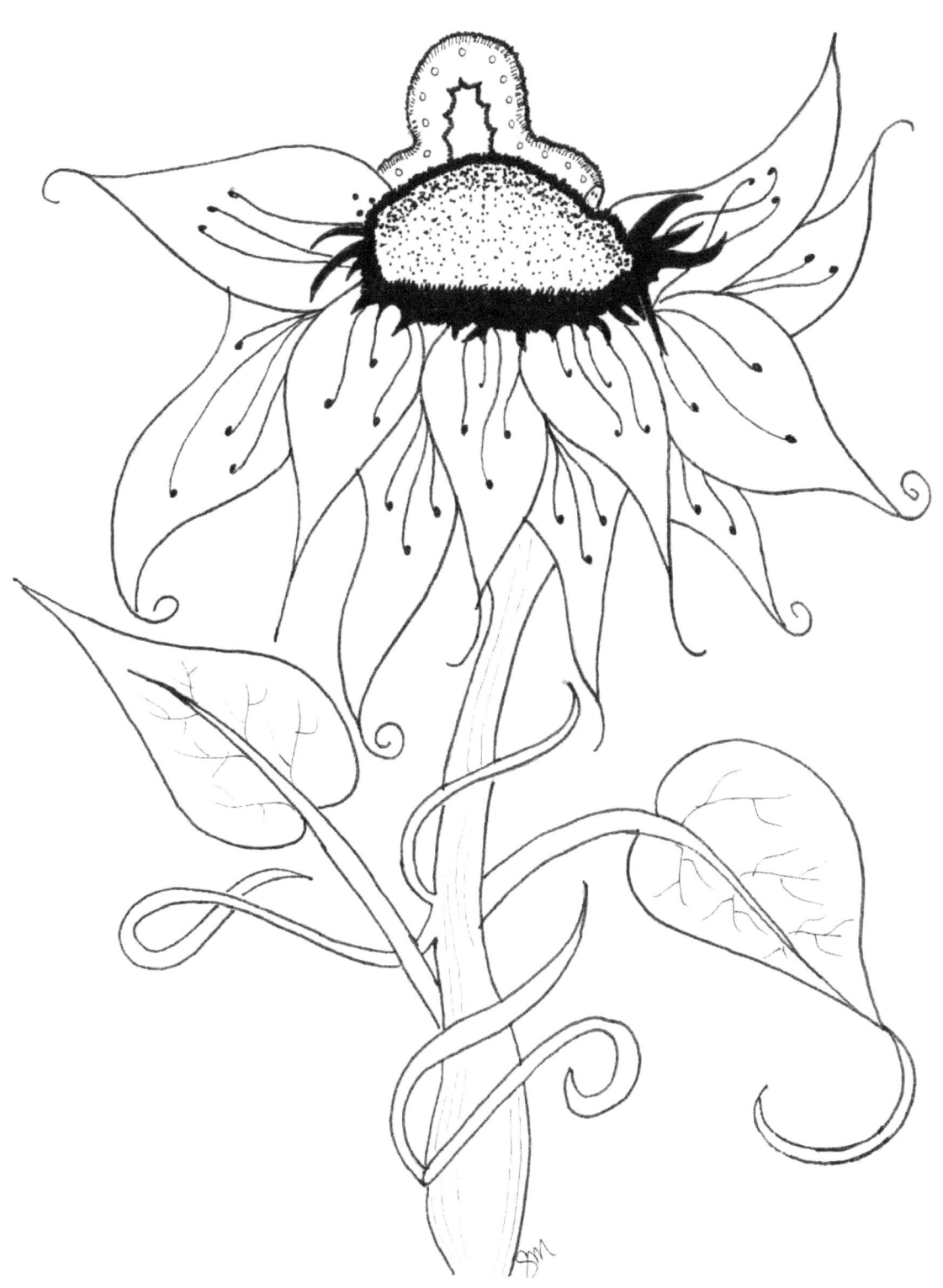

Now
the Lord God
had formed out
of the
ground
all the
wild animals and
all the birds in the sky.
He brought them to
the man to see what
he would name them;
and whatever
the man called
each living creature,
that was its name.

Genesis 2:19

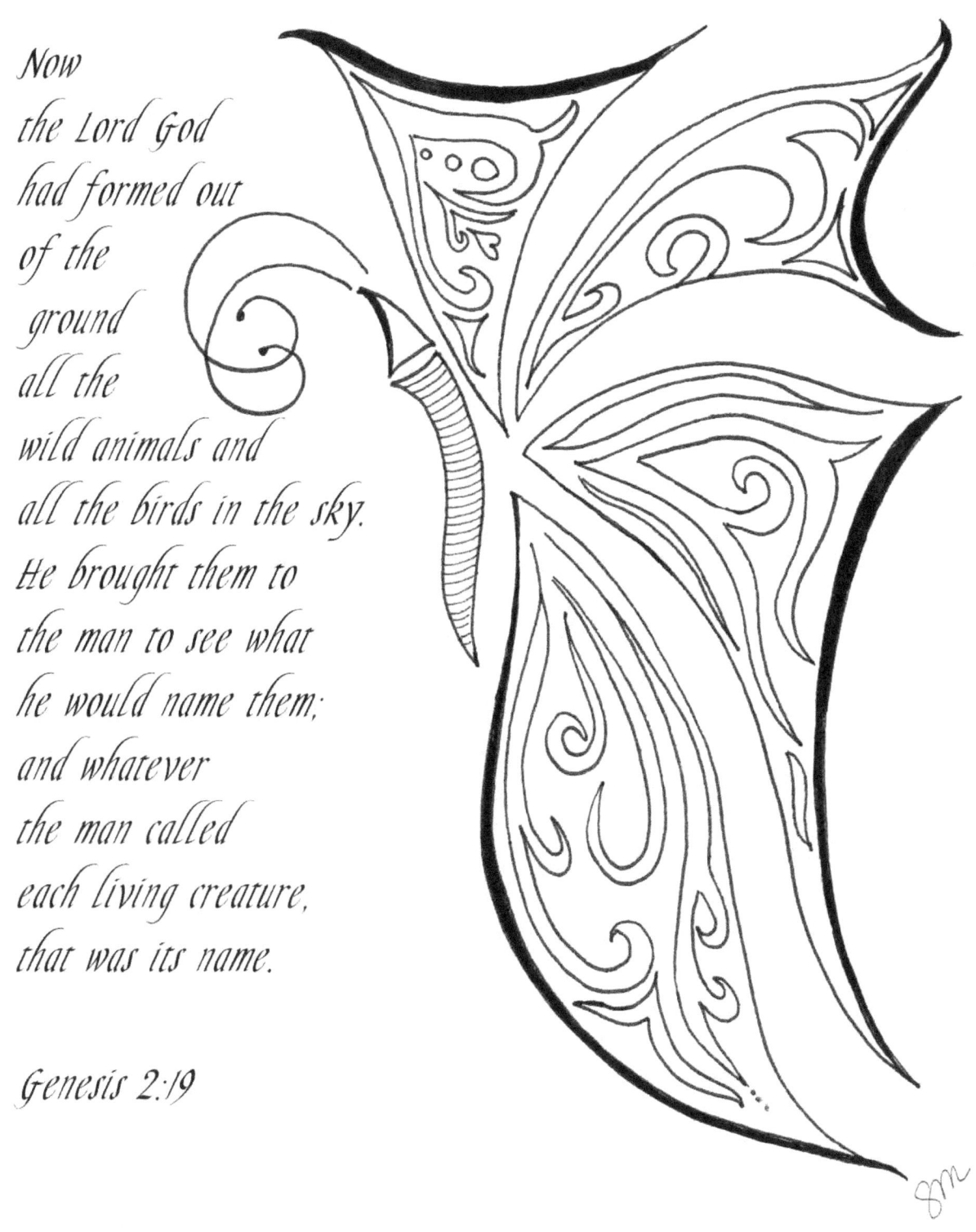

Listen,
I tell you a mystery:

We
will
not all
sleep,
but we
will all be
changed.

1 Corinthians 15:51

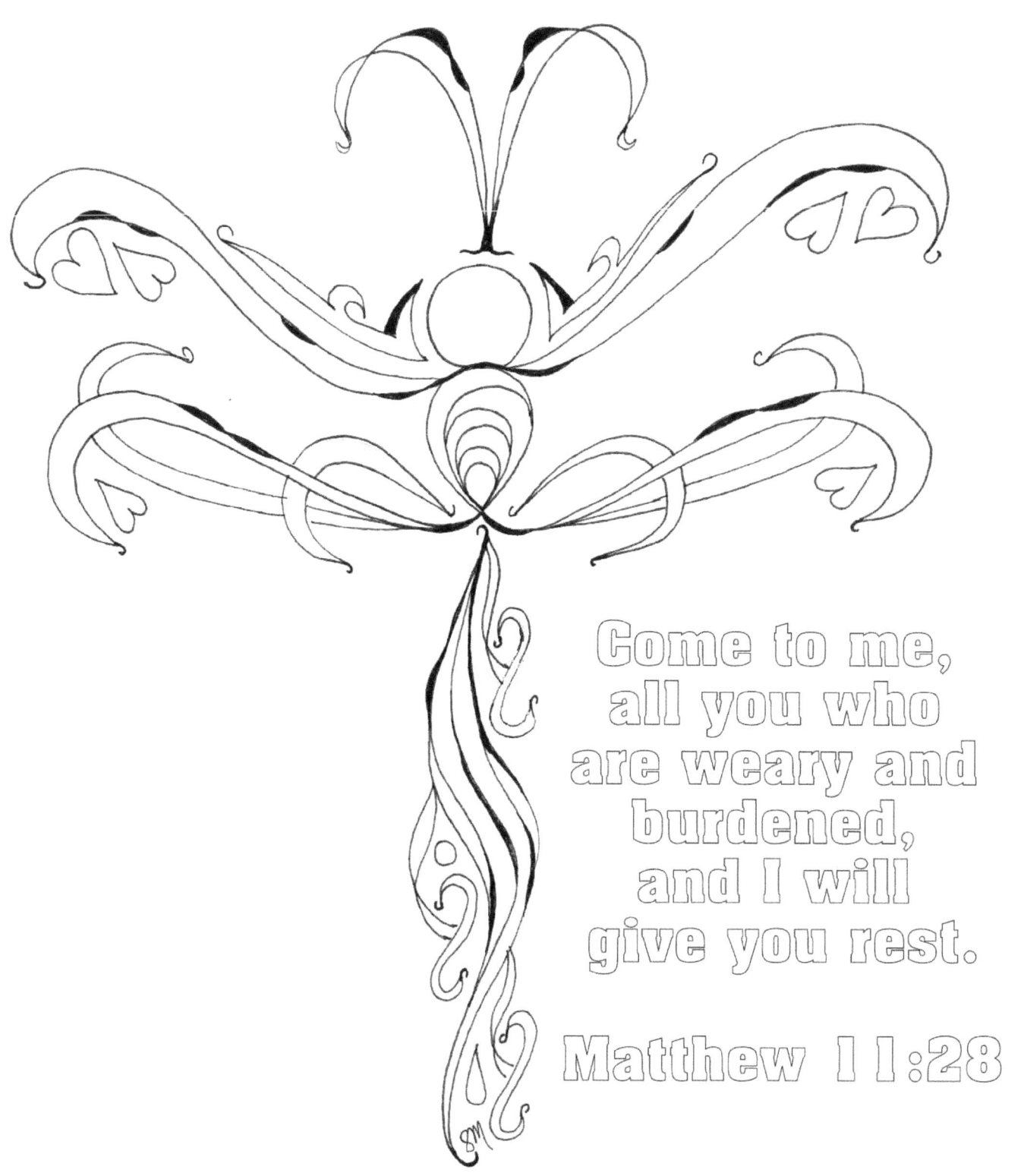

Come to me,
all you who
are weary and
burdened,
and I will
give you rest.

Matthew 11:28

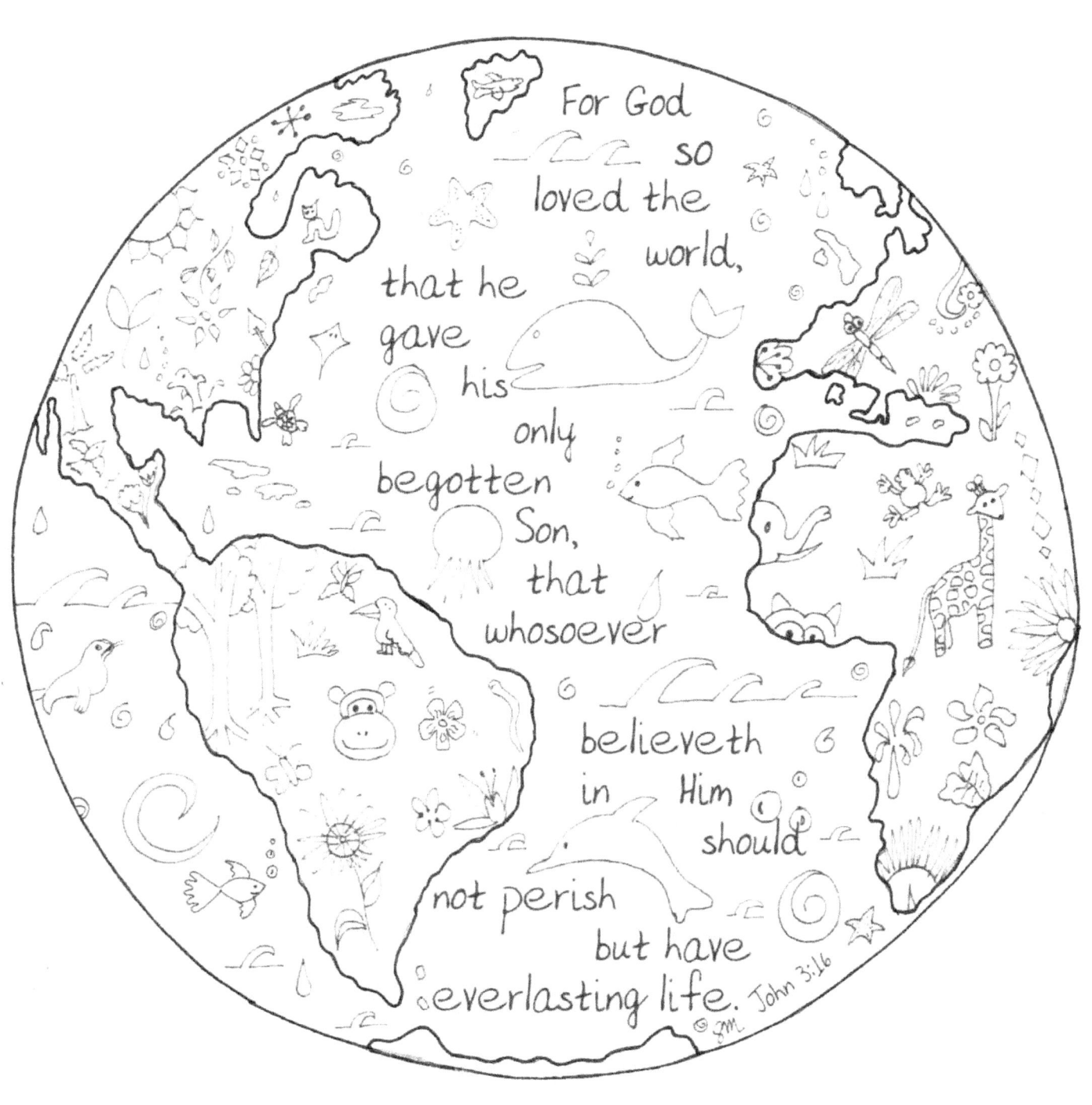

For God so loved the world, that he gave his only begotten Son, that whosoever believeth in Him should not perish but have everlasting life. John 3:16

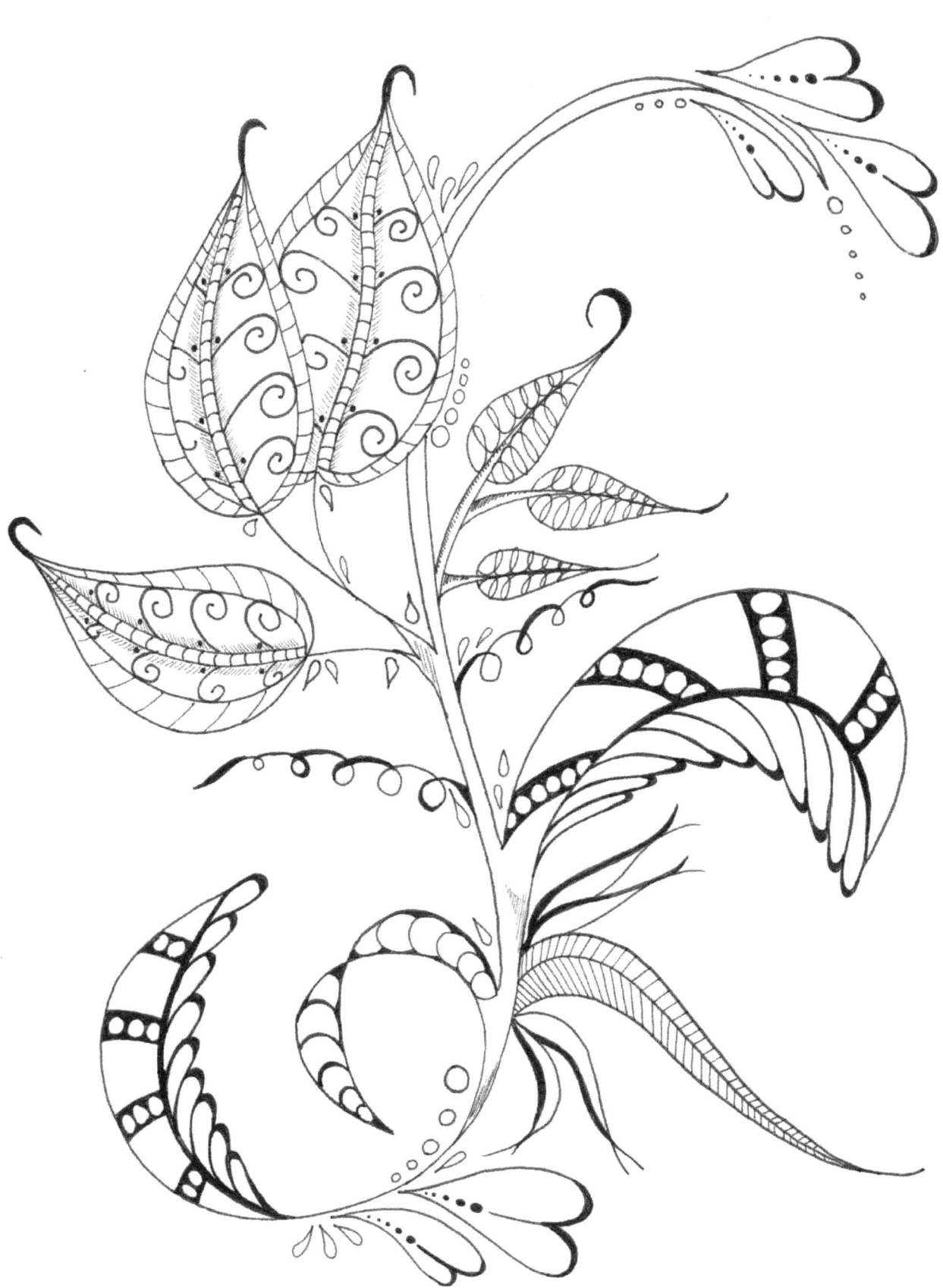

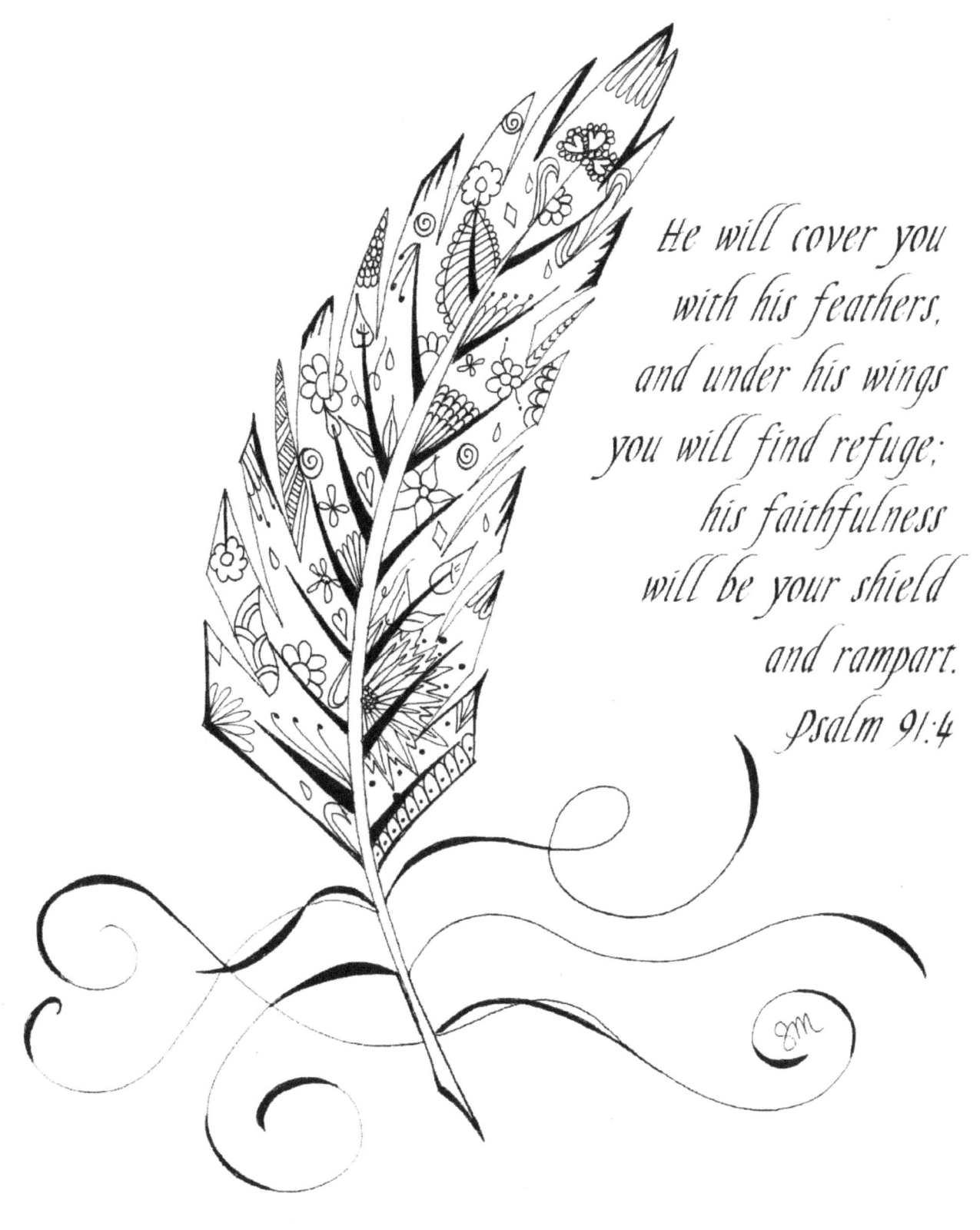

He will cover you
with his feathers,
and under his wings
you will find refuge;
his faithfulness
will be your shield
and rampart.
Psalm 91:4

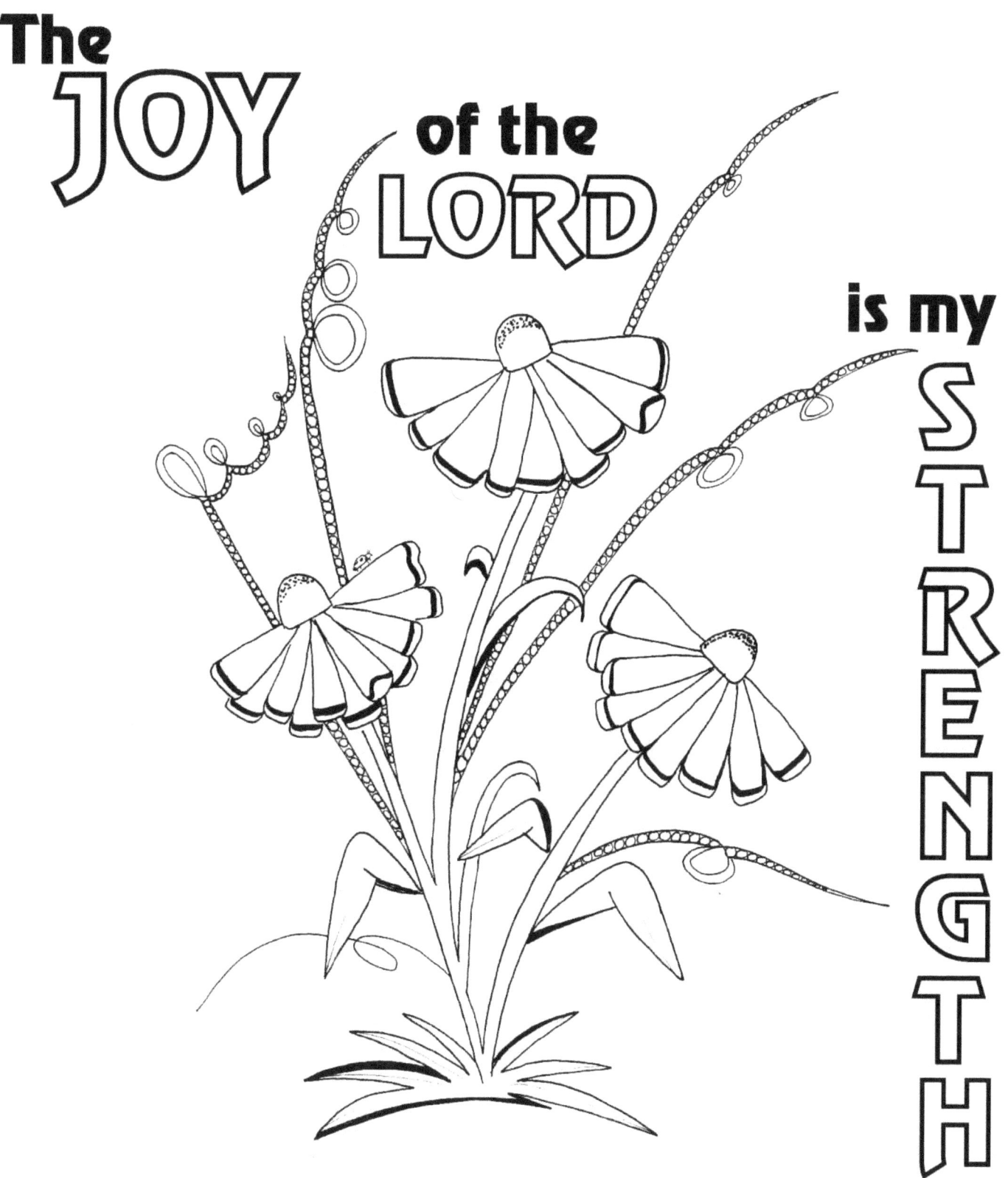

The JOY of the LORD is my STRENGTH

Nehemiah 8:10

How many
are your
works,
Lord!

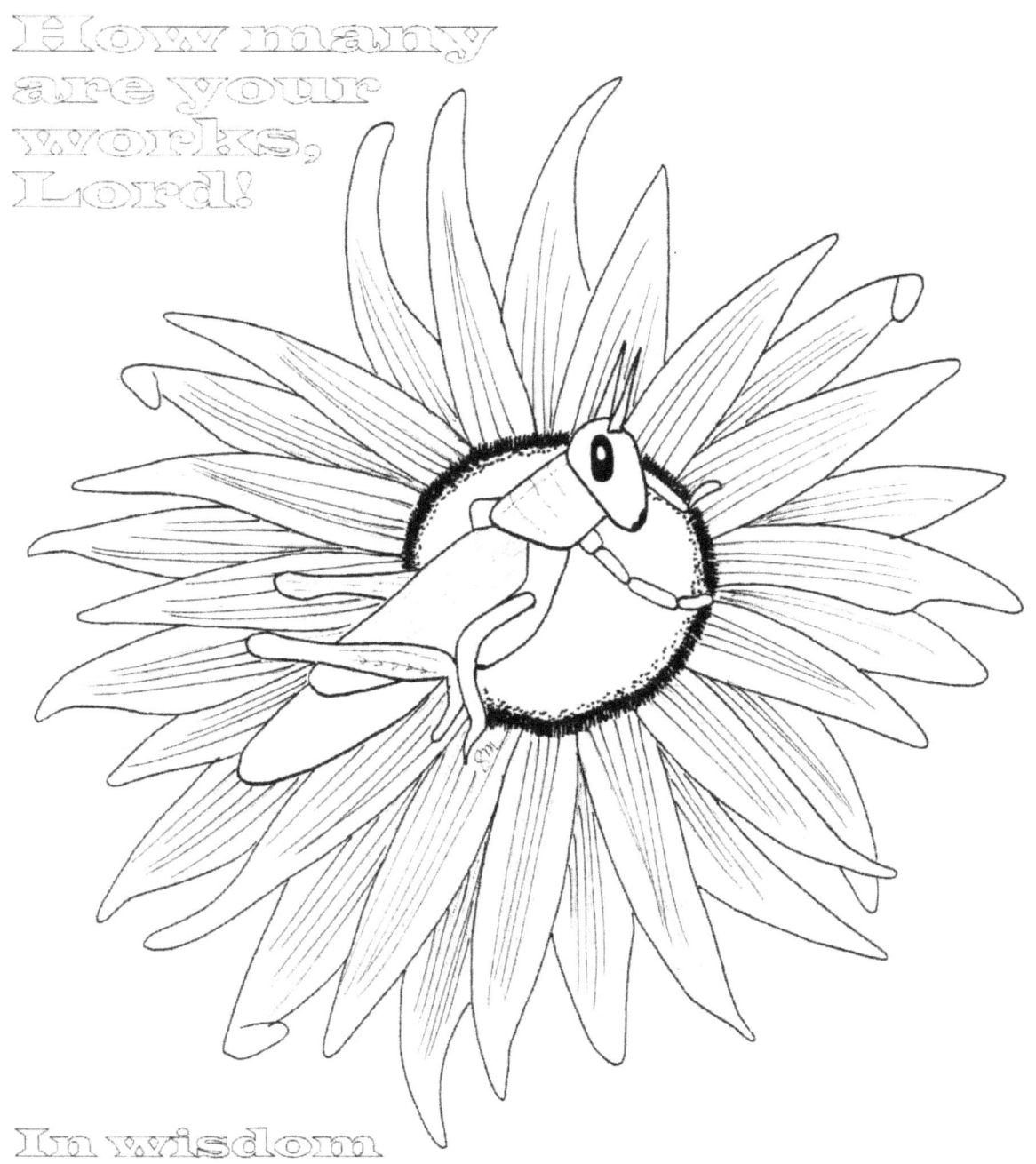

In wisdom
you made them all;
the earth is full
of your creatures.

Psalm 104:24

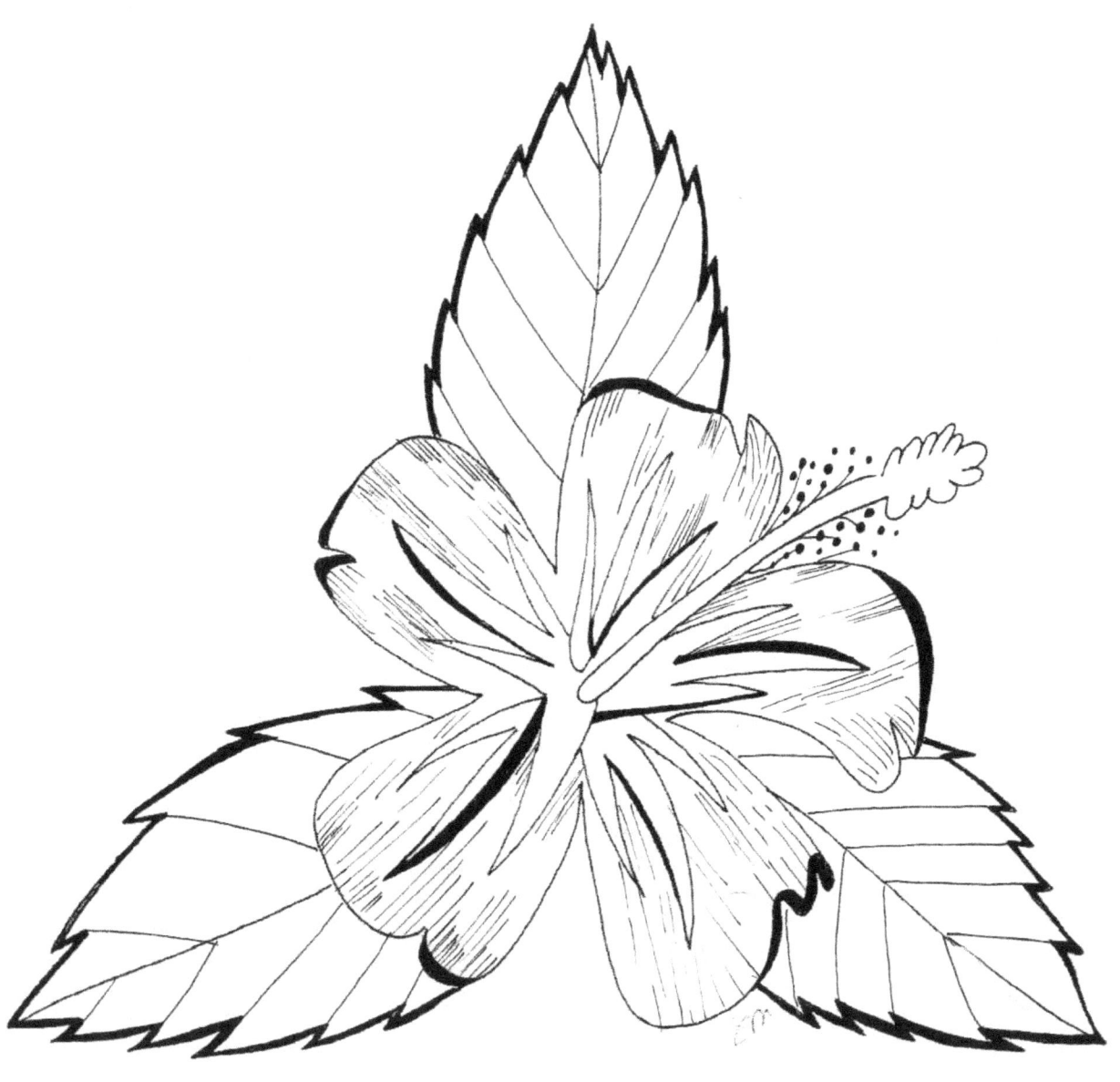

Flowers appear on the earth;
the season of singing has come.
Song of Solomon 2:12

The earth is the Lord's,
and everything in it,
the world, and all
who live in it.

Psalm 24:1

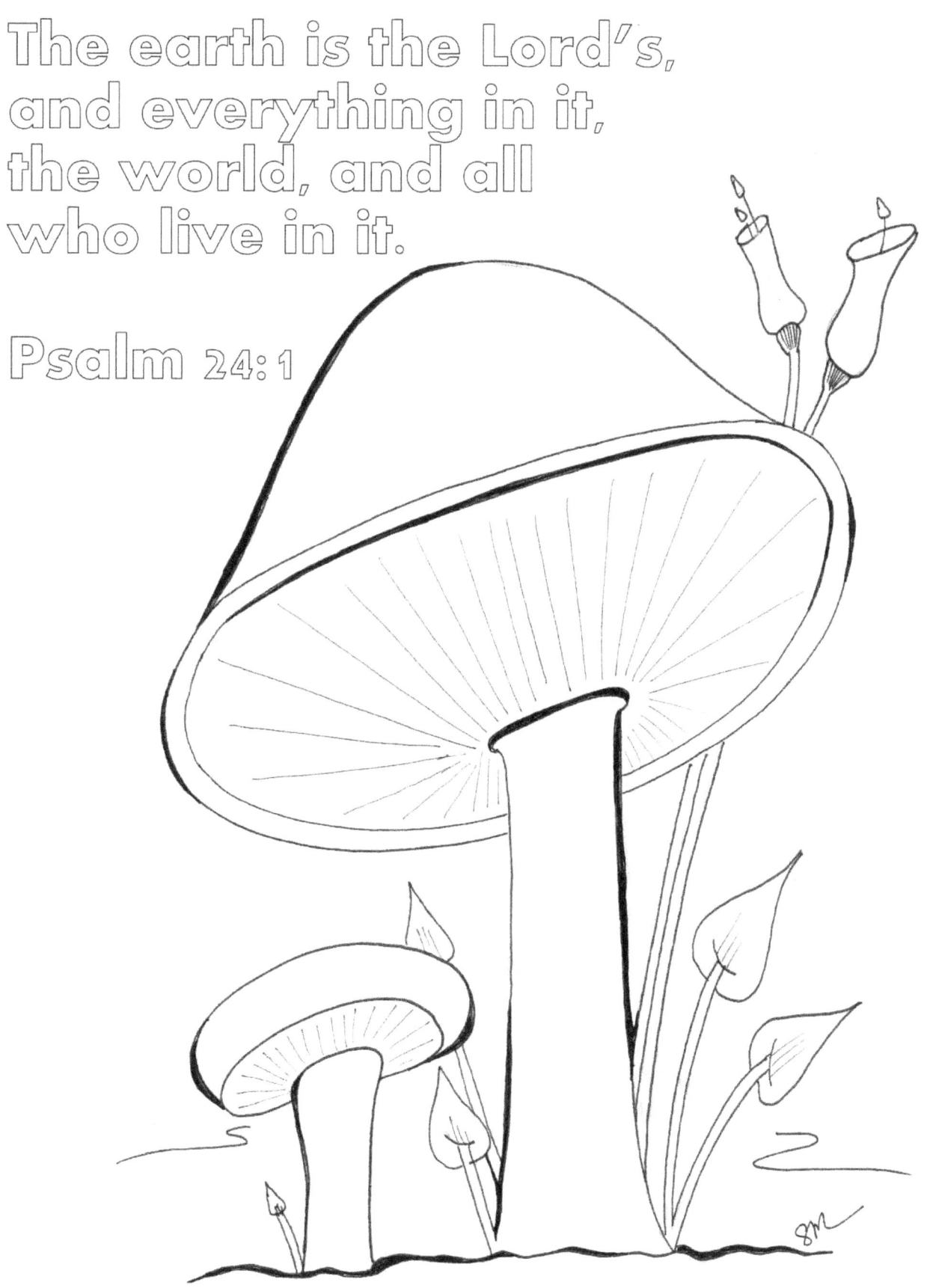

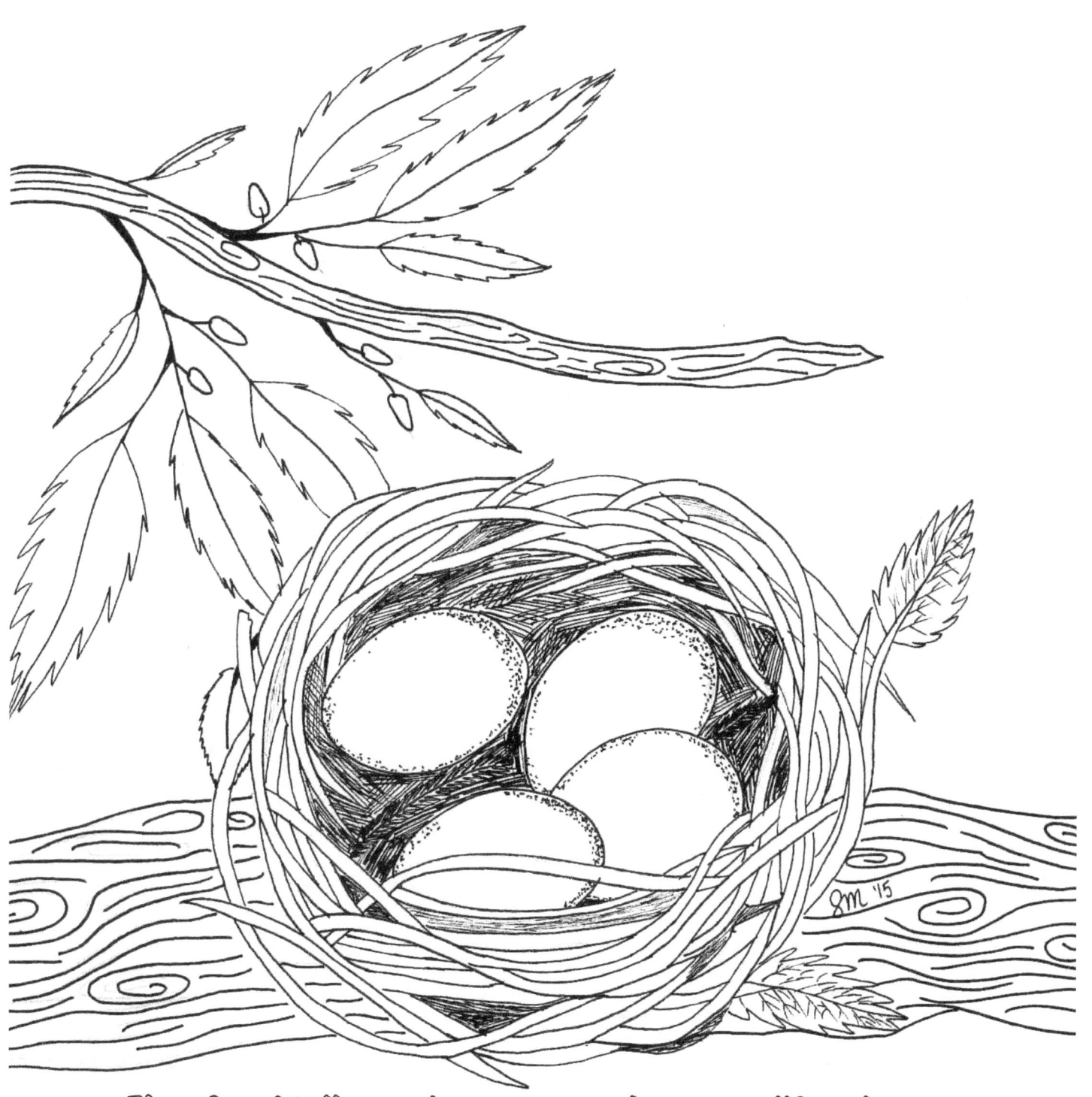

Therefore I tell you, do not worry about your life, what you will eat or drink; or about your body, what you will wear. Is not life more than food, and the body more than clothes? Look at the birds of the air; they do not sow or reap or store away in barns, and yet your heavenly Father feeds them. Are you not much more valuable than they?   Matthew 6: 25-26

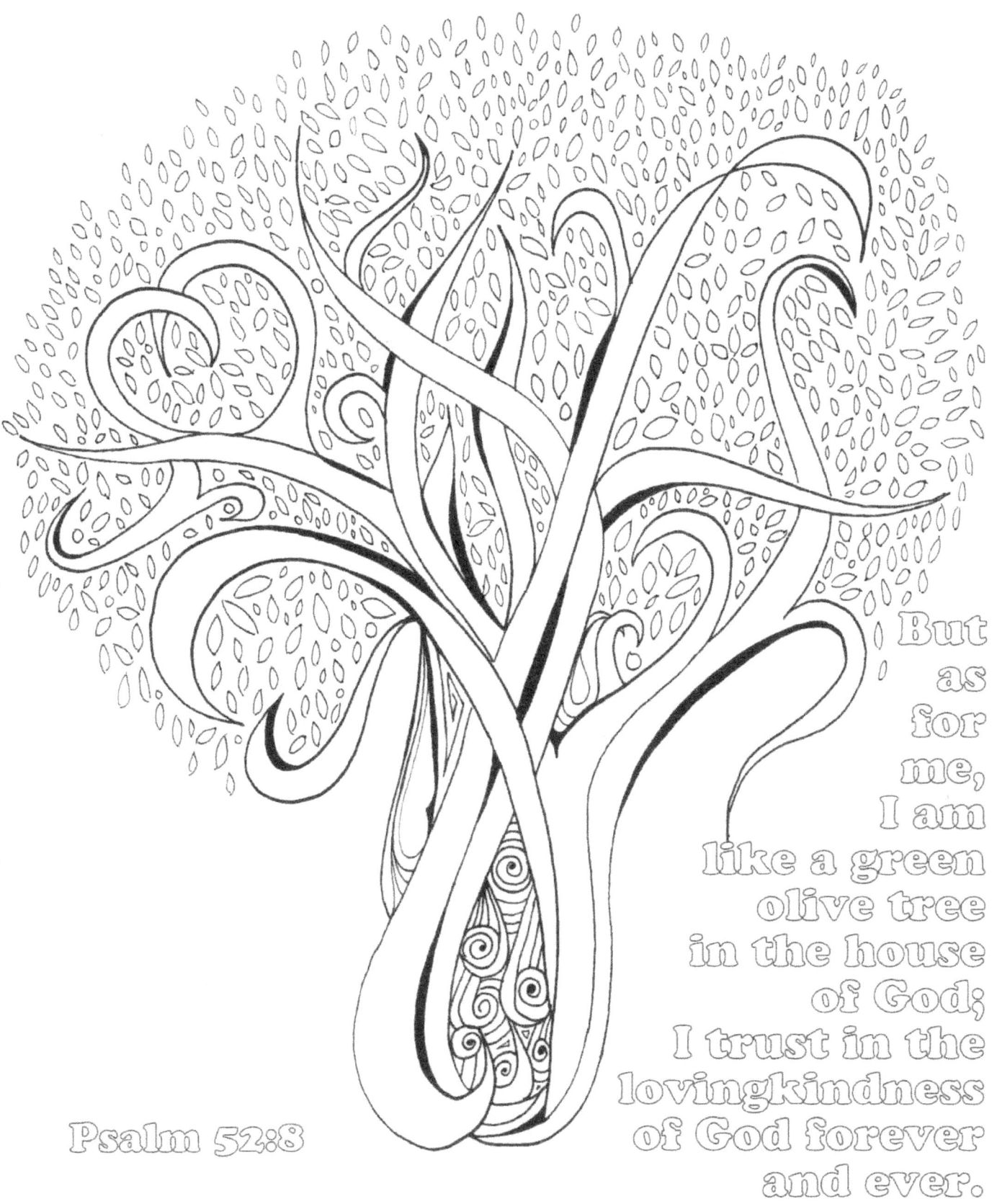

But as for me, I am like a green olive tree in the house of God; I trust in the lovingkindness of God forever and ever.

Psalm 52:8

Look at the birds of the air;
they do not sow or reap
or store away in barns,
and yet your
heavenly Father
feeds them.
 Are you not
much more valuable
than they?

Matthew 6:26

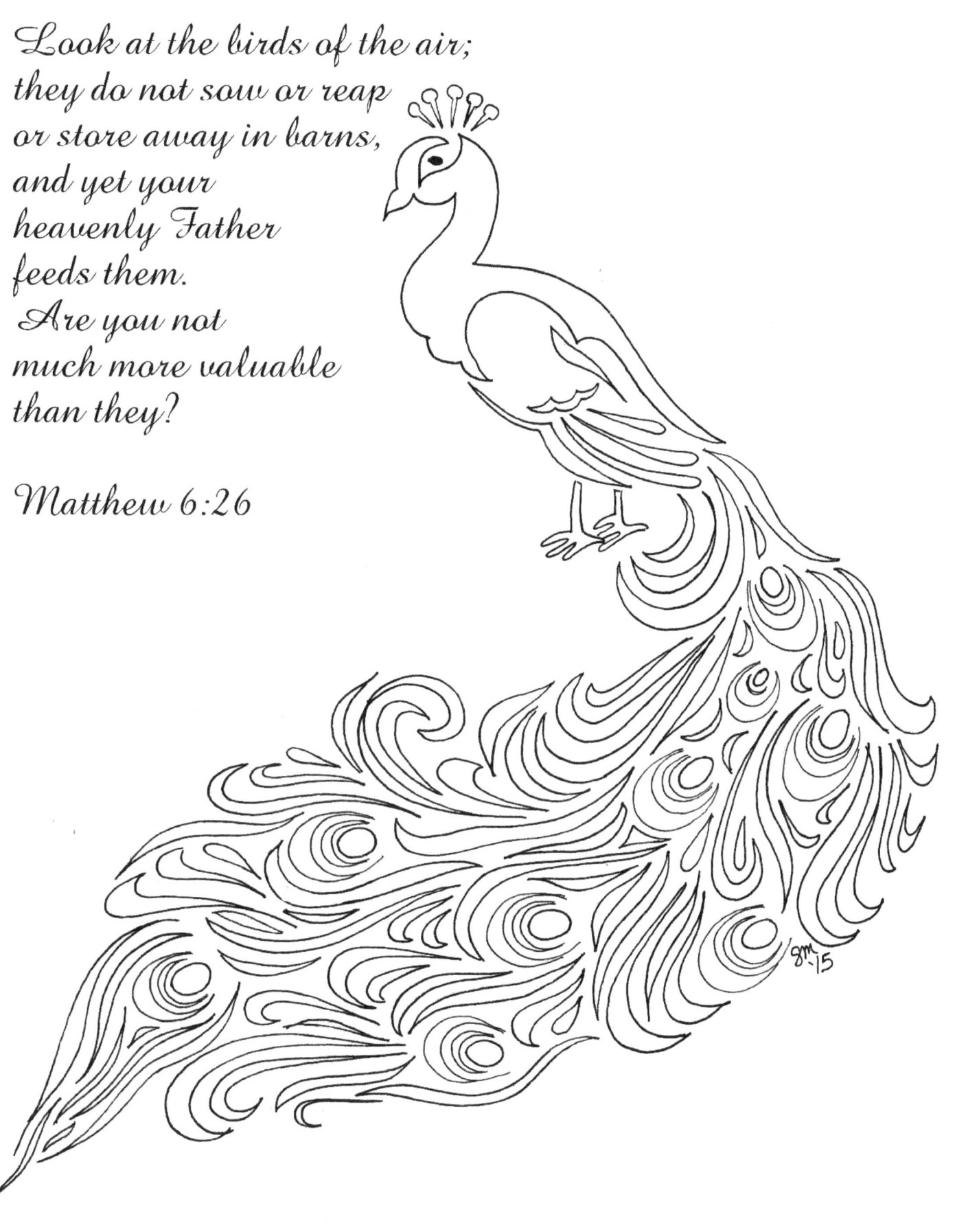

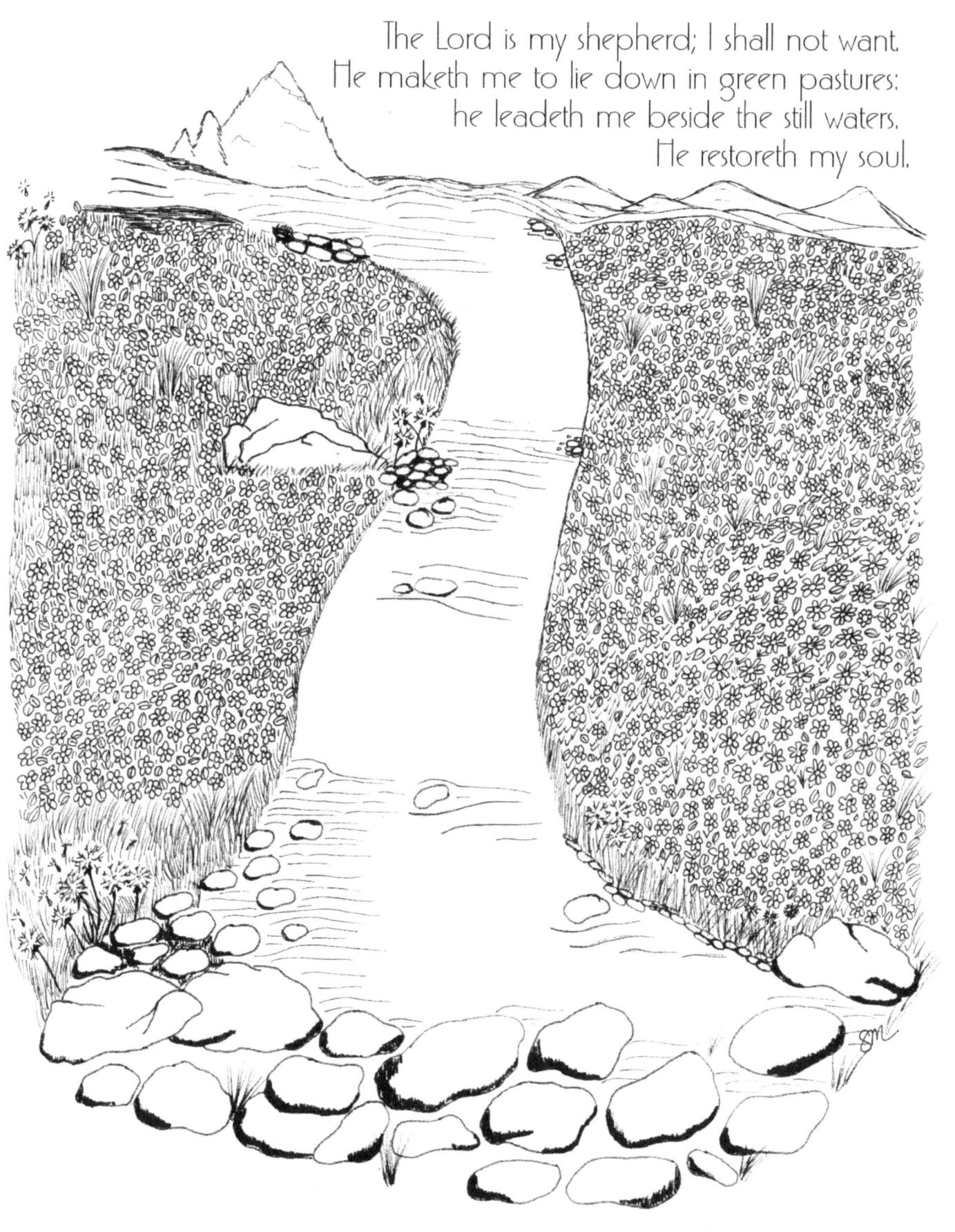

The Lord is my shepherd; I shall not want.
He maketh me to lie down in green pastures:
    he leadeth me beside the still waters.
        He restoreth my soul.

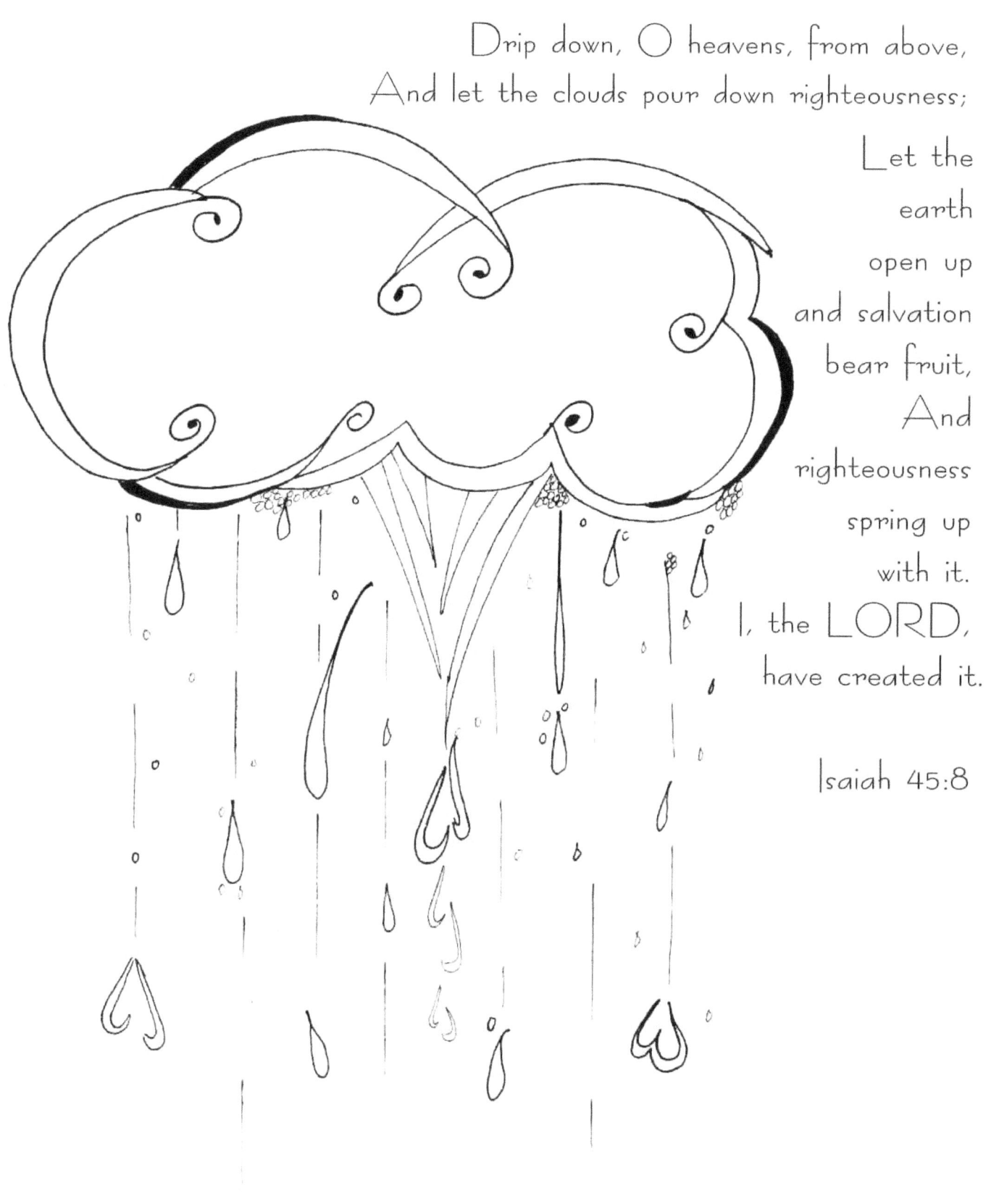

Drip down, O heavens, from above,
And let the clouds pour down righteousness;
Let the
earth
open up
and salvation
bear fruit,
And
righteousness
spring up
with it.
I, the LORD,
have created it.

Isaiah 45:8

THE LORD WILL
FIGHT
FOR
YOU;

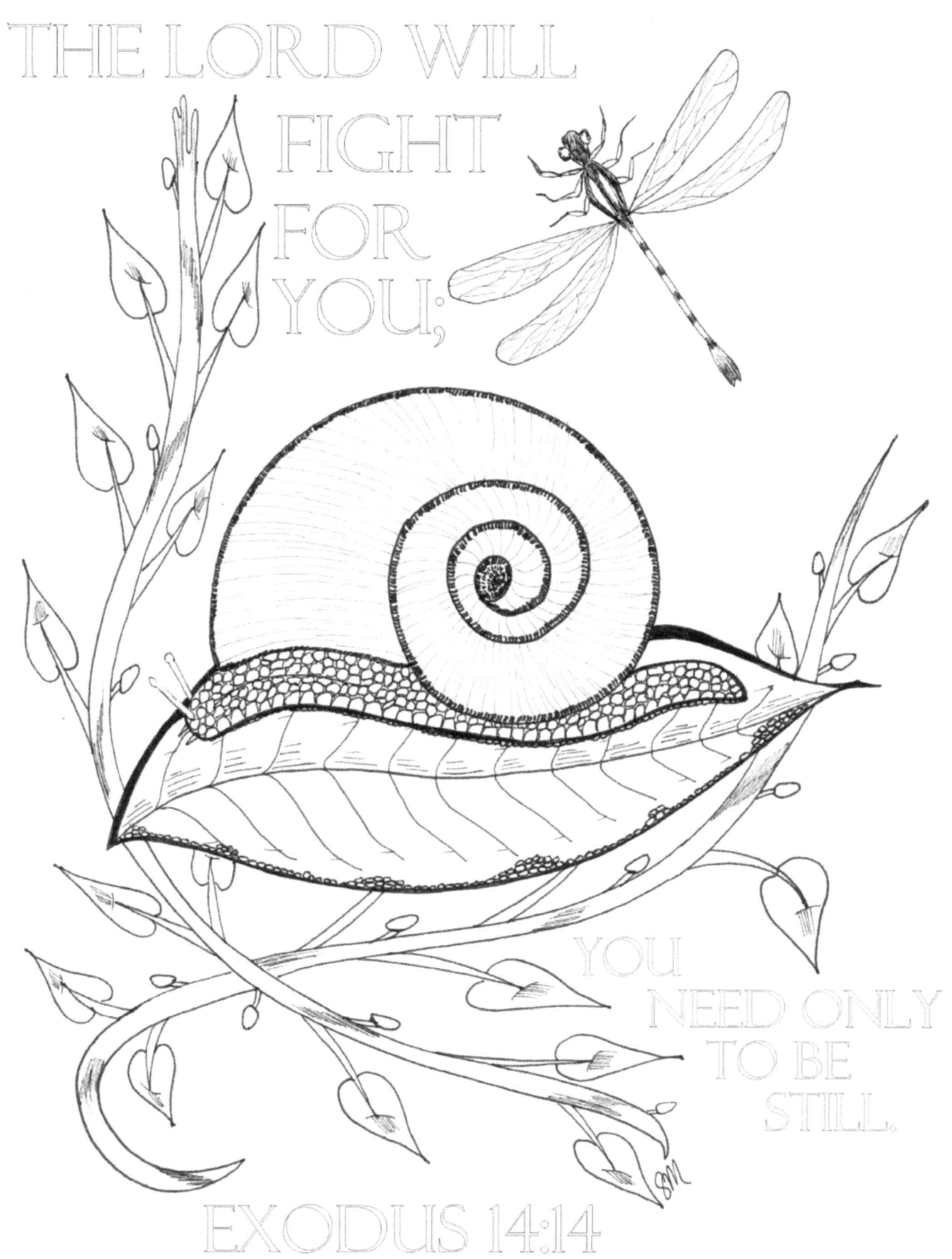

YOU
NEED ONLY
TO BE
STILL.

EXODUS 14:14

He determines the number of the stars

and calls them each by name. Psalm 147:4

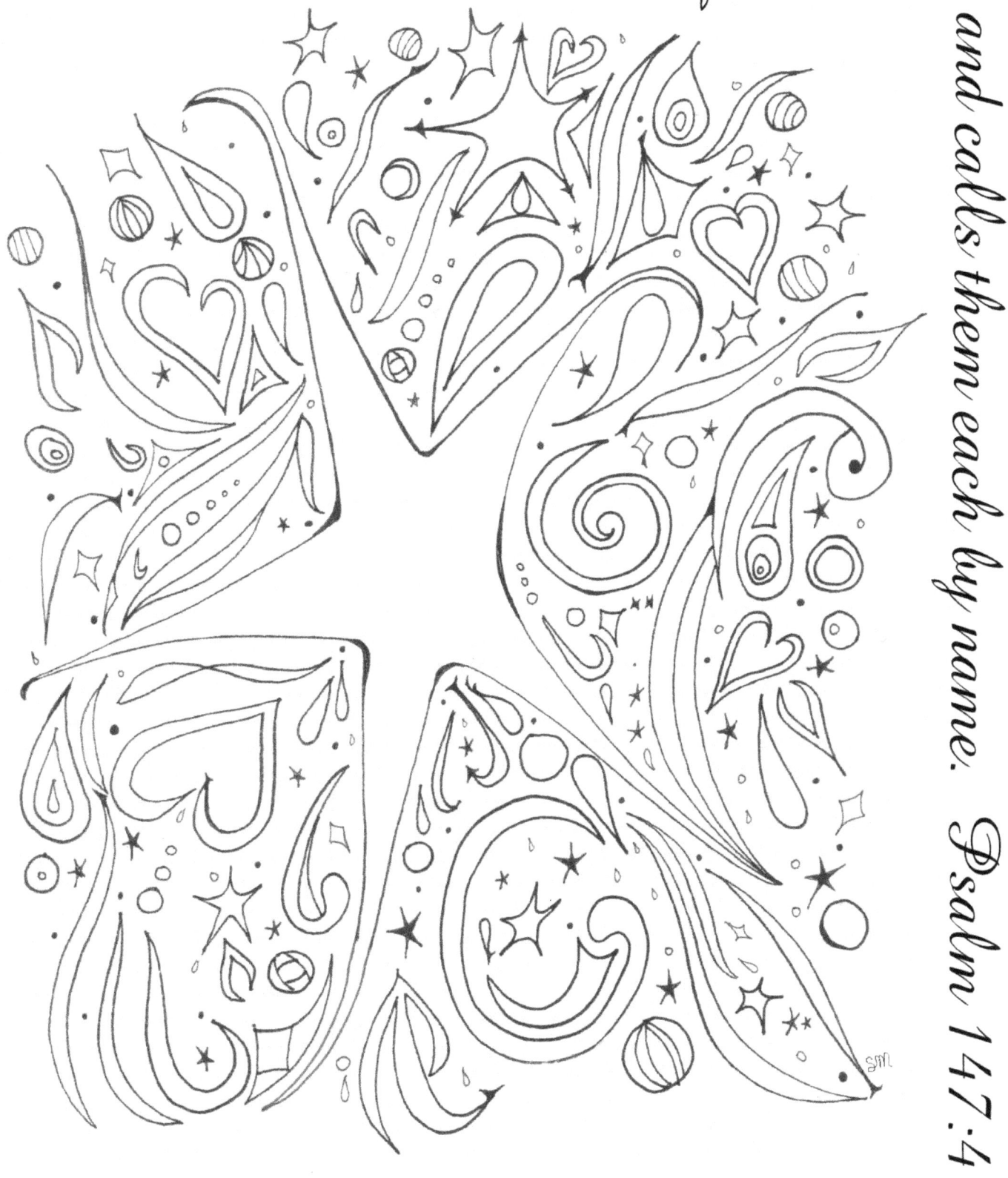

From the rising of the sun to the place where it sets, the name of the Lord is to be praised.

Psalm 113:3

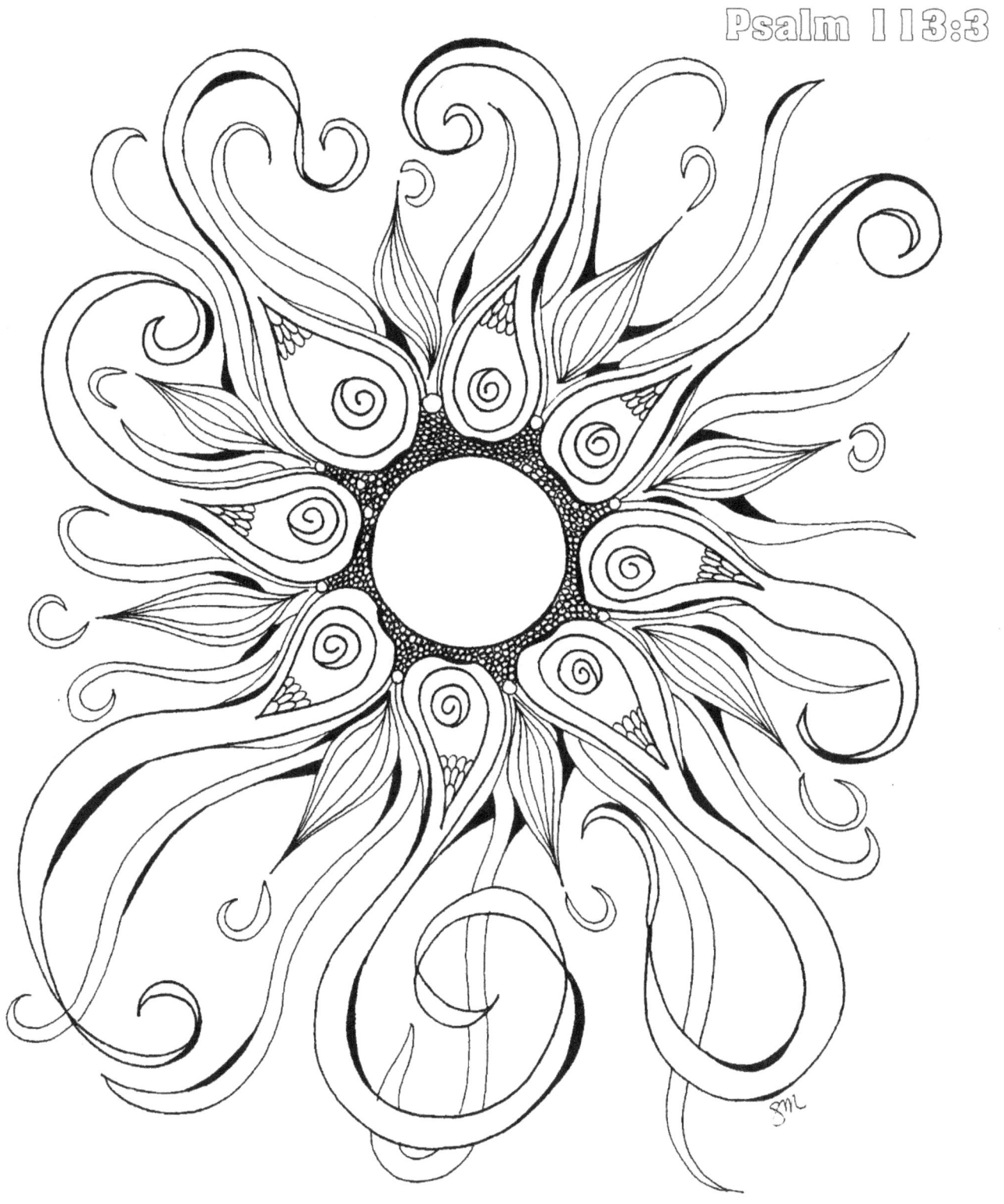

...for with the measure you use,
      it will be measured to you.

Luke 6:38

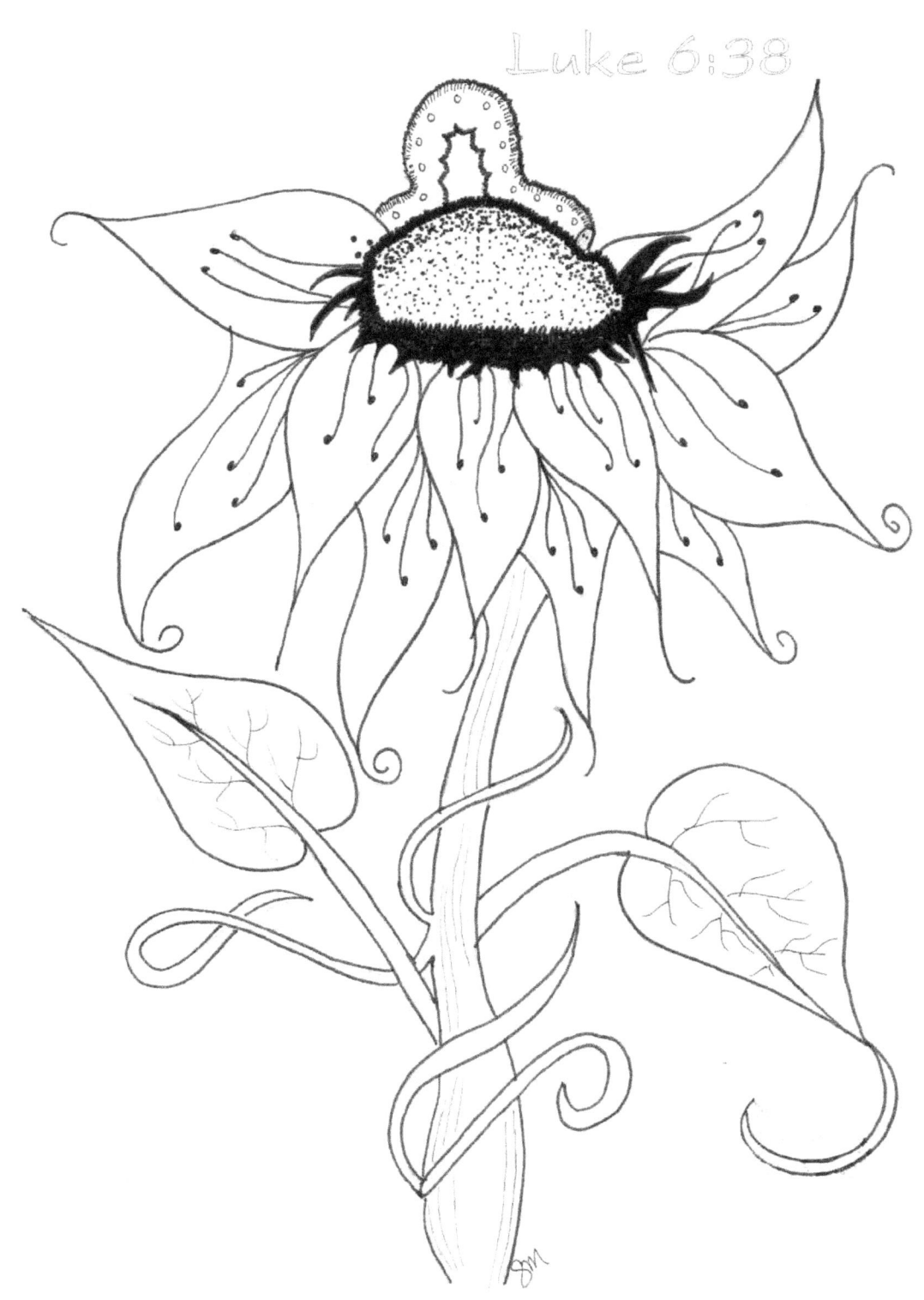

BUT WHOEVER DRINKS THE WATER I GIVE THEM
WILL NEVER THIRST.
INDEED, THE WATER
I GIVE THEM WILL
BECOME IN THEM A
SPRING OF WATER
WELLING UP TO
ETERNAL LIFE.

1 JOHN 4:14